Understanding Bitcoin for Noobs

Christopher McCall

DEDICATION

This book is dedicated to the enigmatic Satoshi Nakamoto, the hardcore cypherpunks, and dedicated miners, developers, and HODLers, who are changing the world as we know it.

CONTENTS

DISCLAIMER

This book should not be taken as, and is not intended to provide, legal or investment advice. This is simply an explanation from a beginner's perspective of the world of Bitcoin and its "ecosystem" for informational purposes only. Please conduct your own thorough research and seek appropriate financial guidange before investing in any cryptocurrency. As stated explicitly on the official Bitcoin website, "the investment in Bitcoin can lead to loss of money over short or even long periods. The investors in Bitcoin should expect prices to have large range fluctuations. The information published on the Website cannot guarantee that the investors in Bitcoin would not lose money."

1 BITCOIN, BLOCKCHAIN, AND CRYPTOCURRENCY

What is Bitcoin? Depending on whom you ask Bitcoin is a currency, a store of wealth, or even "a fraud." What is indisputable is that Bitcoin was created in 2008 when a paper titled Bitcoin: A Peer-to-Peer Electronic Cash System was posted to a cryptography mailing list. The paper was authored by a group or individual calling themselves Satoshi Nakamoto. Over the years there have been many educated guesses as to the true identity of Satoshi Nakamoto, but so far it remains a mystery.

Satoshi Nakamoto's paper created the first successful cryptocurrency through the use of a distributed blockchain - or a continuously growing list of records that act as a public ledger for all transactions. Instead of a central bank or agency controlling the ledger, the blockchain is maintained by a global network of individually owned computers. Because of this, once a transaction is recorded in a block the data cannot be altered retroactively without the alteration of all subsequent blocks, which would require the collusion of at least 51 percent of the total computing power making up the Bitcoin network. It has been estimated that in order to create a single counterfeit Bitcoin transaction it would require approximately $1 billion dollars worth of equipment and additional $1 billion dollars a day in electricity.

Bitcoin and the many electronic currencies that have followed are called cryptocurrenices, because they do not exist in physical form, but are digital currencies which use encryption techniques to regulate the generation of new "coins" and verify the transfer of funds.

New coins are created when they are "mined" by the computers (usually purpose built mining "rigs") that are completing the complicated math problems that are required to run the blockchain. The very first Bitcoin came into existence in January 2009 when the first block or "genesis block" was mined by Satoshi Nakamoto for a reward of 50 Bitcoins. Since that time, the "reward" for successfully mining a block has been reduced by half every 210,000 blocks until the final total of 21 million Bitcoins will have been created.

Bitcoins (abbreviated BTC) are divisible into smaller

units called a Satoshi (named in honor of Satoshi Nakamoto). One Satoshi is one hundred millionth of a Bitcoin (0.00000001 BTC). Originally, the plural for Satoshi was simply Satoshi, however, it is increasingly more common to use Satoshis. As the value of a single Bitcoin increased it became more common to refer to transactions in terms of Satoshis instead of fractions of a Bitcoin.

The first documented commercial transaction involving Bitcoin occurred on May 22nd, 2010 when a programmer from Florida named Laszlo Hanyecz paid 10,000 Bitcoins for two pizzas. Each year, cryptocurrency enthusiasts celebrate the anniversary as "Bitcoin Pizza Day."

CHRISTOPHER MCCALL

2 HOW CAN I GET MY OWN BITCOIN

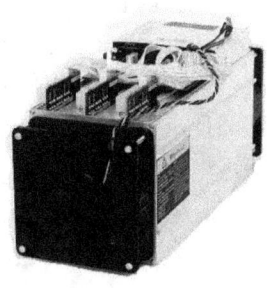 

Bitcoin can be obtained basically one of two ways. You can become a Bitcoin miner and earn the cryptocurrency a little at a time depending on how much computing power and electricity you can afford to dedicate to it, or you can purchase Bitcoin. It is also possible to earn Bitcoin by trading it, or accepting it as payment for a transaction - or even to solicit it as a donation. However, most of the people investing in Bitcoin today do so by purchasing it on an "exchange." There are numerous exchanges around the world, where you can buy and sell Bitcoin in various local currencies.

One of the biggest and fastest growing exchanges in the United States is Coinbase. Founded in 2012, Coinbase is an digital asset broker based in San Francisco, California. As of November, 2017 Coinbase had an estimated 13,300,000 users and has received investment from the likes of the New York Stock Exchange and USAA.

Exchanges give the look and feel of a traditional bank or brokerage, but they are distinctly different. While convenient, unlike a US bank, your cryptocurrency holdings are not insured by the FDIC. If someone hacks your account and steals your Bitcoin, it is probably gone forever. Different exchanges offer different levels of protection to try to prevent this from happening, but if you are planning on investing any money through an exchange you need to educate yourself on what the best exchange is for your individual needs as well as to continuously educate yourself about advanced online security precautions.

3 WALLETS AND EXCHANGES

Regardless of how you plan on obtaining your Bitcoin, you will need some place to store it. Bitcoin is stored in "wallets." Wallets are basically just an account number or serial number which denote who owns the Bitcoin recorded on each transaction of the blockchain. Each wallet has a "public key" which is like a serial number or account number. When you buy, or someone sends you Bitcoin (or any other of the Bitcoin type currencies) they send it to your wallet using your public key. You can enter your public key at any number of "block chain explorer" websites and it will show how much Bitcoin that wallet holds and every transaction associated with that key. All of that information is publicly visible. That is ok, because that "wallet" is relatively anonymous, and just about the only thing anyone can do with that public key is to send you Bitcoin.

Each wallet also has a "private key." This needs to be kept 100 percent top secret. It is basically a really long password that you use to send Bitcoin from your wallet to someone else. Anyone who knows that key can send your Bitcoin to any other wallet (ie steal it or sell it etc). That transaction will be completely irreversible and almost impossible to trace.

Online wallets and mobile wallets allow you to send or receive Bitcoin without much hassle. They are fairly straight forward, but some allow you to keep control of your private keys while, others keep control over those keys, instead providing you with a list of words that must be entered in a certain order to back up or restore your wallet if you lose or replace your phone.

Exchanges are usually not really wallets. Typically, you only know the public keys that it generates for you. When you buy or receive Bitcoin you have it sent to one of the almost unlimited public keys you can generate when logged into your account. However, you do not know the private keys and your Bitcoin really isn't held in your "wallet." It is more like when you deposit cash into your bank checking account - they keep the money and credit you with that amount. When you withdraw it or spend it, they send out Bitcoin they hold and then deduct the amount from your account. With an actual wallet you are controlling the actual Bitcoin as it is recorded on the block chain.

Receiving Bitcoin is usually free for both wallets and exchanges. Sending Bitcoin from a wallet costs a fee based on how big the transaction is. That size isn't the value of the transaction, it is the actual size in bytes of the code in the block chain required to records that transfer. So, in theory, a $10 transaction can cost the sender as much as a $1 million dollar transaction depending on the data size of the transactions.

When using an exchange to buy or sell Bitcoin they usually charged a fee based on the value of the transaction. There is usually a minimum fee for small transactions and as the amount you buy or sell gets larger that percentage usually decreases, so a $4 purchase may cost almost as much in fees as the amount of Bitcoin purchased, but a large purchase may be relatively cheap.

CHRISTOPHER MCCALL

4 PAPER WALLETS

For many, the ultimate way to guarantee the security of your Bitcoin is to use a "Paper Wallet." A paper wallet is just that - a printed piece of paper that is the only record of your public and private keys.

(An example of a printed paper wallet)

There are many precautions that must be taken when using a paper wallet. For example, if you lose or destroy the paper wallet, your Bitcoin will be gone forever, with no way of ever recovering it. Similarly, if proper security precautions are not taken when creating your paper wallet - or in keeping your private keys private, your Bitcoin is at serious risk as well.

Several reputable websites offer instructions on how to securely create a paper wallet. Paper wallets are usually free to generate, and you can create a practically unlimited amount of them for only the cost of the paper and ink they are printed with. These online resources are subject to change, but should be easy to find and their instructions are usually straight forward. If you are considering using a paper wallet, make sure to do your own research so that it is as up to date as possible.

It should also be noted that paper wallets usually allow you to accumulate and store Bitcoin, etc, but do not let you spend them piece by piece. If you want to spend or cash in coins stored in a paper wallet, it is first necessary to "sweep" that paper wallet into an online wallet or exchange. You must sweep the entire balance of paper wallet into the new wallet or exchange and never use that paper wallet again. Most online and mobile wallets have a fairly straight forward process for this and usually feature a "sweep" button or link somewhere easy to find to assist you in this.

5 HARDWARE WALLETS

Considered by some to be the most secure way for an individual to store their cryptocurrency assets is the "hardware wallet." A hardware wallet is a physical piece of equipment that stores the users private keys and must be connected to a computer to complete a Bitcoin transaction.

Hardware wallets allegedly offer the security to conduct your transactions safely, even on a computer that may be compromised by malware. This comes at a price, however, as hardware wallets can be expensive. Furthermore, there have been documented incidents where hardware wallets were vulnerable to hackers. However, hardware wallets can be used interactively as opposed to paper wallets, which as previously mentioned must be "swept" or imported into a software wallet for your funds to be spent.

Two of the most popular hardware wallets currently on the market at the time of publishing are the Trezor Bitcon Wallet and the Ledger Nano S Cryptocurrency Wallet. For a hardware wallet to maintain security, however, it is important to have an as up to date wallet as possible, and to keep up to date on the latest firmware or security updates for your wallet.

6 MINING BITCOIN

Bitcoin and other similar cryptocurrencies can only exist as long as there are enough people (or increasingly companies) willing to dedicate sufficient computing power to process and verify each new Bitcoin transaction and thus maintain the blockchain. These people are called "miners."

Each time a new block is created, the miner is rewarded with newly created Bitcoin. At inception the reward consisted of 50 new Bitcoins. However, every 210,000 blocks the reward is cut in half, until a final total of 21 million Bitcoins will have been created. After that point, miners will solely be rewarded by payment of the transaction fees that are charged to record a Bitcoin transfer.

In the early days of Bitcoin, most mining was done on a personal computer using the CPU to complete the mathematical calculations required to verify a new block. As more computing power joins the Bitcoin network, the "difficulty" of solving a block is changed to maintain a fixed rate of approximately one new block every 10 minutes. As a result, most mining today is done with specialized, purpose built "mining rigs" often working together as part of a mining "pool."

Factors such as your miner's electrical consumption, processing power (called Hash Rate), the current mining difficulty, and current block reward are crucial for determining the profitability of any mining operation, large or small.

An Antminer S9 by Bitmain

As of this writing, arguably the most state of the art Bitcoin miner is the Antminer S9 manufactured by Bitmain. The Antminer is an ASIC (Application Specific Integrated Circuit) based machine whose only purpose is processing the SHA-256 hashing algorithm used to find blocks in the Bitcoin blockchain. The S-9 has a processing speed of a staggering 13.5 terahashes per second.

The cost of the Antminer or comparable Bitcoin miner can be in the thousands of dollars, and during times of higher profitability may not even be in stock for purchase. Before you purchase your miner, however, there are many simple online calculators that will help you determine if you can make a profit mining Bitcoin with your intended equipment.

As a rule of thumb, when Bitcoin is more valuable, mining is more profitable. When the price of Bitcoin declines you may find that you are spending more on electricity and equipment costs than you can make in return.

CHRISTOPHER MCCALL

7 MINING POOLS

Once you have made the decision to start mining Bitcoin, you will probably want to join a mining pool. Mining pools allow miners to share their processing power over a network and then split the rewards based on the amount of work each miner contributed. Mining pools vary on their payout schedule, but most of them send your earnings to your designated wallet once a day and/or after you have accumulated a threshold amount of Bitcoin.

Joining a mining pool is usually pretty straight forward. Typically, you create a new account with a user name and password. Then you create a "worker" for each piece of mining equipment you want to use with the pool. If you have one Antminer, for example, you create one worker. Depending on your specific miner, you then enter the pools address in your miner configuration along with your username and miner name to tell your miner to begin mining with that pool.

The very first mining pool created was SlushPool (www.slushpool.com). Unlike most of the largest mining pools today (which are all based in China), SlushPool is based in the Czech Republic. It uses a SCORE based reward system which is proportional to the amount of work completed, but weighted by the time submitted.

One of the largest mining pools in the world is China based Antpool (www.antpool.com). Run by Bitmain, the manufacturer of the Antminer series of Bitcoin miners, Antpool offers a choice of reward systems that the miner can choose from based on whether they desire a more consistent, predictable reward, or if they want their reward based solely on the work performed (even though you may earn less on some days and more on other days depending on pool luck, etc).

There are many other pools out there to consider as well, and it may be desirable to try a couple pools for a week or so each to determine which pool you like best.

GLOSSARY

Bitcoin
> Defined by its inventor as "A peer-to-peer electronic cash system," Bitcoin was the world's first cryptocurrency.

Blockchain
> A digital ledger which records every transaction of a cryptocurrency adding a new block to the existing chain as new transactions are recorded and verified.

Cryptocurrency
> A digital currency which uses encryption to regulate the creation of "coins" or units as well as to verify transactions, using a publicly distributed ledger instead of a central bank or regulating government agency.

Ecosystem
> Much like a natural ecosystem, the Bitcoin Ecosystem is the environment in which Bitcoin exists. It includes miners, traders, investors, consumers, wallets, exchanges, and the merchants who accept Bitcoin as payment.

FOMO

FOMO, or the Fear of Missing Out is a quasi-psychological phenomenon that sometimes influences people to act impulsively or rashly, when buying or selling Bitcoin.

FUD

Sometimes contributing factor to FOMO, Fear Uncertainty and Doubt, which is sometimes fostered or evoked intentionally to manipulate an position of advantage.

HODL

Originally derived from a typo, HODL now stands for Hold on For Dear Life, reminding Bitcoin enthusiasts to resist the temptation of selling as the value of their Bitcoins rises.

Key

A series of numbers and letters that act like an account number or password to control your Bitcoin. There are two types of keys:

Public Keys can be publicly shared and act like an account number for verifying or receiving Bitcoin.

Private Keys are like passwords that control the Bitcoin and allow it to be spent or transferred. Private Keys should always be considered Top Secret, because anyone who knows the private key has complete, irreversible control over that Bitcoin.

Mining

Bitcoin mining is the process of maintaining the blockchain of Bitcoin transaction history. It is also the process by which Bitcoins are created, as new Bitcoins are given as a reward for creating new blocks of the blockchain. However, the creation of new coins is capped at a maximum of 21 million, at which point mining will be rewarded solely by transaction fees charged for recording Bitcoin transactions to the blockchain.

Noob

A noob is a newcomer or newbie, who is inexperienced, particularly when referring to computers or the internet.

Satoshi

The smallest divisible fraction of a Bitcoin. One Satoshi is one hundred millionth of a Bitcoin (0.00000001 BTC).

Wallet

A wallet can be a computer program, mobile app, website, computer device, or simply a printed piece of paper that stores they keys which control ownership of your Bitcoin. Electronic wallets simplify the process of sending and receiving Bitcoin.

ABOUT THE AUTHOR

Christopher McCall is an entrepreneur, author, and Bitcoin enthusiast. Having run one of the first computer Bulletin Board Systems out of his bedroom in the early 1980s the world of Cryptocurrency was immediately appealing. Like many people, he believes in only "buying what you know" and has since dedicated himself to learning as much about Bitcoin as he possibly can.

www.ingramcontent.com/pod-product-compliance
Lightning Source LLC
Chambersburg PA
CBHW030040230526
45472CB00002B/599